Letterland

Phonics Activity Book 3

My name is

Let's learn about...

u oo oy oi

aw au

ou ow

About Letterland

Letterland is an imaginary place where letters come to life! The friendly Letterland characters help children to easily understand the sound and shape of letters – one of the key skills needed when learning to read and write.

Simple stories about the Letterland characters explain letter sounds and shapes, so that confusion over similar looking letters is avoided and children are motivated to listen, think and learn.

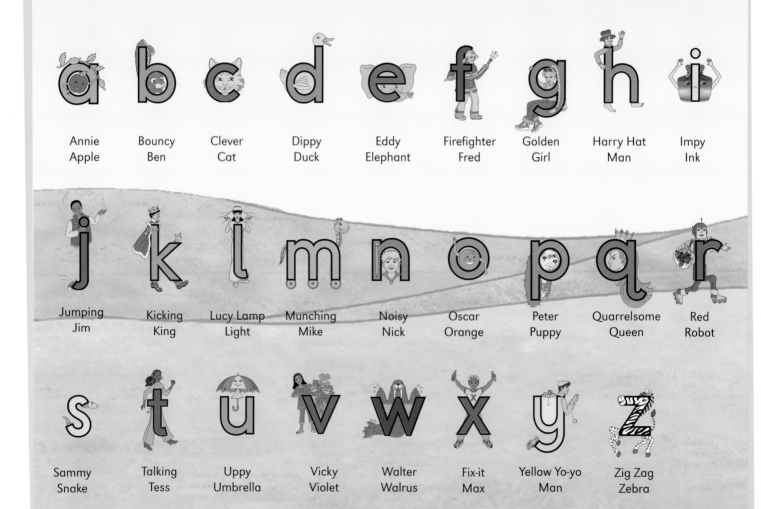

| Annie Apple | Bouncy Ben | Clever Cat | Dippy Duck | Eddy Elephant | Firefighter Fred | Golden Girl | Harry Hat Man | Impy Ink |

| Jumping Jim | Kicking King | Lucy Lamp Light | Munching Mike | Noisy Nick | Oscar Orange | Peter Puppy | Quarrelsome Queen | Red Robot |

| Sammy Snake | Talking Tess | Uppy Umbrella | Vicky Violet | Walter Walrus | Fix-it Max | Yellow Yo-yo Man | Zig Zag Zebra |

For more information, including a pronunciation guide for all the letter sounds, see: **www.letterland.com**

How to use this book

Letterland stories give child-friendly reasons why, when certain letters come together, they make a completely new sound. On each page, read the Spelling Story and talk about the Letterland characters and the reasons for their change of sound. Your child will quickly discover how easy it is to remember the new sound just by learning the story reason for it. For more fulsome versions of the stories, you might like to look at our *Phonics Touch and Spell* book or the titles *Beyond ABC* and *Far Beyond ABC*.

Note: A 'digraph' is two letters representing one sound. e.g. **sh**op

Study the pages together with your child. Each time start by reviewing the previous digraphs, to practise their sounds before focusing on the next pages. The aim is for your child to respond without hesitation with the correct sound for each digraph.

Stickers

Award stickers as you go along. You may also like to start a Digraph scrap book using the character stickers from *Phonics Activity Books* 3 to 6. Look out for words to collect under each of them. Where you see this icon, you will need stickers to complete the exercise.

Skills covered include:
- phonemic awareness
- decoding skills
- word building
- reading for meaning
- sentence completion

It is important to use this *Phonics Activity Book*:
- when children are not tired
- when there are no background distractions
- for short periods of time
- with plenty of praise and encouragement.

Left-hander

Finger tips 4cm from tip of pencil

Paper side edge
30°
Table edge

Paper side edge
20°
Table edge

Right-hander

Finger tips 2cm from tip of pencil

Upside Down Umbrella

When umbrellas get pushed into their letter shapes upside down they don't make their usual sound. Hear the 'u' sound in words like p**u**t, p**u**ll and b**u**sh.

1. Write the word for each picture. Then write the word that rhymes below each one.

push	pull	bull	bush

_____   _____

_____   _____

2. Read the sentences and write one of these words in the spaces.

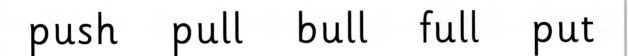

push   pull   bull   full   put

The farmer told us that the barn was _____ so we had to _____ and _____ the _____ in the snow. We _____ it in a shed.

The Boot and Foot Twins

When the Boot Twin takes the Foot Twin's boots and the F**oo**t Twin accidentally steps in a puddle, he cries out, '**Oo**! Just l**oo**k at my f**oo**t!'

1. Link **oo** to the words that contain their sound. Write the words in the spaces. Cross out the other pictures.

hood

2. Read the sentences and write one of these words in the spaces.

| took   looks   Hood   cooked   shook |

The girl _____ a cake from the tray.

The food is cold and not _____.

The man shivered and _____.

He _____ like Robin _____.

3. Fill in the missing words to complete the sentence.

Five, good _____

on a _____ en

bookshelf.

7

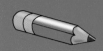

1. Read the sentences. Then colour the star next to the matching picture.

The cup is full.

He likes pudding!

2. Put these puzzle pieces together to make three longer words to write on the lines below.

foot   book

under   ball

cook   stood

_____

_____

_____

3. Match the sounds of **oo** with the Boot or Foot Twin. Write the words in the spaces.

| food | cook | soon | good | took | smooth | zoo | wood |

Boot Twin

_____

_____

_____

_____

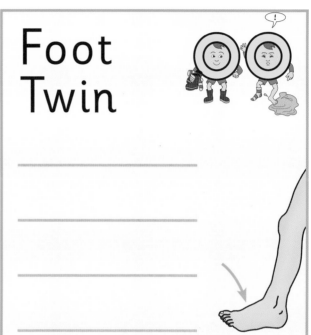

Foot Twin

_____

_____

_____

_____

4. Look at the picture and fill in the spaces with the correct word. Then read the sentence out loud.

| pulled pushed |

Ben _____ on Peter.

Peter _____ on Clever Cat.

Clever Cat _____ on a carrot.

A boy called Roy and Yellow Yo-yo Man

There's a boy called Roy in Letterland, who enjoys leaping over an 'o' into Yellow Yo-yo Man's sack. They shout '**oy**!' as he leaps.

1. Write **oy** on the lines. Read the words and match them to the pictures.

t__ __s   •   •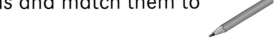

b__ __s   •   •

s__ __   •   •

2. Cross out the word that does not sound right in the sentence. Trace over the one that does.

The toy / toil box was almost full.

3. Read the sentences and write the sentence under the picture that matches. Cross out the sentence that does not match a picture.

Roy will enjoy his new toy.

Let's avoid those boys.

The robot toy can pick up coins.

_____

_____

_____

_____

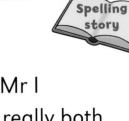
Spelling story

In a few words you will find Roy playing his game with Mr I. Then Mr I pretends to be annoyed, but they really both enjoy making a n**oi**se, '**oi**!'

1. Write **oi** on the lines. Read the words and match them to the pictures.

b __ l •

  •

c __ ns •

 •

p __ nt •

 •

t __ let •

 •

2. Cross out the word that does not sound right in the sentence. Trace over the one that does.

She put an egg in the pan to boil.
boy

I need to go to the coin
toilet.

3. Draw a line around all the **oi** words in the word search below. They go across and down.

a	t	o	i	l	e	t
c	o	i	n	s	a	b
y	i	g	o	e	h	o
e	l	t	i	f	s	i
a	d	s	s	o	i	l
g	a	i	e	e	t	w

coins

toilet

soil

oil

noise

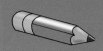

1. Fill in the missing words to complete the sentences.
The words you need are in the box below.

annoyed   boy   toys   voyage

This _____ is _____.

The _____ are on a

space _____.

2. Look at the pictures and write a word underneath each picture
to match.

_____ _____ _____ _____

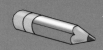
3. Read these sentences and colour the stars next to the matching pictures.

The toilet flush is very noisy.

The boy scout found some pound coins.

4. How many coins can you count below? Write the number in the box.

coins

Annie Apple and Walter Walrus

When Walter Walrus is about he splashes Annie Apple with salty water. She cries out, '**Aw**! Don't be so **aw**ful!'

1. Colour in Annie Apple and Walter Walrus. Then write **aw** on the lines. Read the words and match them to the pictures.

dr___ •   •

s___ •   •

p___ •   •

Marvellous! Delightful! Keep it up! Perfect!

Wonderful! Hooray! Excellent! You did it!

You're a star!

Super job!

Good for you!

You know your sounds!

Fantastic!

 u  oo oo  oy

 oi  aw  au

 ou  ow

Letterland

Letterland

2. Read the two words beneath each picture. Circle the word that matches the picture.

straw stove   hawk hawl   lawn yawn

3. Fill in the missing words to complete the sentences.
The words you need are in the box below.

| draw   paw   saw   strawberry |

The vet ＿＿ that the cat had hurt it's ＿＿.

Dippy can ＿＿ a ＿＿＿＿.

17

Annie Apple and Walter Walrus

When Walter Walrus is feeling n**au**ghty, he fills Uppy Umbrella's letter with water and splashes Annie Apple from there. She cries out again, 'Aw! Don't be n**au**ghty!'.

1. Label this autumn scene with the **aw** and **au** words below.

saucer   paw   saw   yawn   straw   jigsaw

2. Write a word for each picture below.

| launch   saucer |

A cup and _____

A rocket _____

3. Read and trace the words below. Then draw the picture in the box.

autumn	astronaut

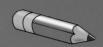

1. Read the sentences. Then colour the star next to the matching picture.

This jigsaw has paw prints on it.

He did not use a straw to drink his strawberry milk.

The astronaut is now an author.

They all applauded the new show.

2. Read the sentence. Look at the four other words and see if you can substitute one or two words to make a new sentence.

| Let's find a clean saucer. | straw | jigsaw | get | new |

3. Underline all the **aw** and **au** words in the instructions below. Then complete the picture.

Draw claws on the cat's paws.
Then draw a rocket launch in the sky.

4. Underline all the **aw** and **au** words in the story. Read it to a friend.

We went to see a rocket launch. We had to wait a long time so we did a jigsaw. We yawned, and then fell asleep.

When we woke up the rocket had launched! Aw! That's awful!

Oscar Orange and Walter Walrus

Spelling story

Watch out when you see an orange next to Walter Walrus. When Walter splashes salty water in Oscar's eyes Walter also bumps his chin and they both h**ow**l, '**Ow**!'

1. Colour in Oscar Orange and Walter Walrus. Write **ow** on the lines. Read the words and match them to the pictures.

__ __ l •   •

c __ __ s •   •

br __ __ n •   •

2. Add **er** to each word and write it under the picture.

show

flow ⟶ **er**

tow

_____   _____   _____

3. Complete the sentences using the **ow** words below.

| brown   cow   shower   towels |

The _____ are by

the _____ .

This ___ is white

and _____ .

4. Look at the pictures and write an **ow** word underneath
each picture to match.

_____   _____   _____   _____

.

Oscar Orange and Walter Walrus

Spelling story

When Walter Walrus fills Uppy Umbrella's letter with water and splashes Oscar Orange from there. Walter slips and and we hear them both shouting '**Ou**!' (as in **ou**ch!).

1. Write the word for each picture. Then write the rhyming word below.

| mountain | vowels | pounce |
| bounce | towels | fountain |

_____   _____   _____

_____   _____   _____

2. Which thing makes the **lou**dest noise? Circle it.

3. Label this town scene with the **ow** and **ou** words below.

| mountain | clowns | flowers | fountain |
| mouse | cow | ground | clouds |

4. Look at the picture. Then complete the sentence below.

There is a big _____

in my _____!

1. Read and trace the words below. Then draw the picture in each box that matches its word.

mouse	flower

2. Fill in the missing words to complete the sentence. Cross out the words that do not fit.

sound   cloud   loud   mouse

That _____ is

too _____ !

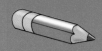

3. Read the sentence and look at the picture clue. Fill in the spaces with the missing words.

| found | clown | round |

The cat dressed up as a
_____ ! She had _____ a
hat and a _____ nose.

Phonic Word Builder

The Letterlanders are coming together to build words! Say their sounds, then blend them together to read the word.

t ow n   town

Sticker time!

Put a book by that bush.
Put a coin by the boy.
Put the cows by the house.
Add a rocket launching up
into space.

Story time!

Read the story once on your own using the picture clues to help you. Then read it again out loud.

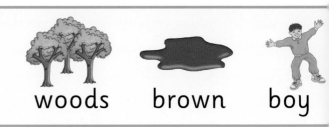

woods   brown   boy

A [boy] went out in the [woods] to take [photos] of the autumn trees that were yellow and [brown]. He took a [photo] but then saw a gold thing on the ground. He crouched down and saw it was a gold [coin] in the [soil]. Wow! He picked it up and put it in his pocket. Then a loud growling sound made him jump. What was it? Was it a [tiger] about to pounce? He ran back to his [house]. "What was that sound?", he shouted.

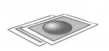 photos coin soil tiger house  cloud

"Oh! I'm glad you came back to the .
Look at that ! That's a thunder
" said Mum.
"I'm glad it was not a  growling!" said
the  .
His mum smiled. " do not hide in
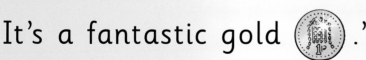!"
"Ha, ha! No, a  in the , Mum!
Look what I did find in the !
It's a fantastic gold ."

Certificate

Well done!

This is to certify that

....

has finished the
LETTERLAND® Phonics Activity Books